HAIR BUSINESS ROADMAP

*Fundamentals To Go From Zero To A
Million Dollar Hair Business*

JULIA W. STRUNK

DEDICATION

I would like to dedicate this book to my loving husband Thomas who has always supported me in my business pursuits.

My wonderful children Amelia and Enzo. My parents Stephen and Veronica and my siblings, Martin, Amos, Kenneth, and Salome.

HERE IS YOUR GOLDEN TICKET: SPECIAL INVITATION

I would like to take this moment to express my gratitude for buying this book and I would like to invite you to my FREE Masterclass on How To Start Your Own Branded Hair Business.

Here is the link to save your spot.

Go here: WealthyHair.com/Webinar

TABLE OF CONTENTS

INTRODUCTION

> *"Change will not come if we wait for some other person or some other time. We are the ones we've been waiting for. We are the change that we seek."*
> — *Barack Obama*

Who Am I?

Hello and welcome to my book! I am Julia Strunk, the founder and president of Wealthy Hair, a successful online hair extension business. I have been selling hair since 2007 and I am excited to share with you my journey and lessons learned going from having never sold hair before to having a million-dollar hair business.

But before I begin telling you about all the secrets of creating your own successful hair extension business, you should know who I am and why you should listen to me.

I am from Kenya, and I moved to the USA to go to college and because I watched The Fresh Prince of Bel-Air

TV show, I thought that wow, I need to go to this magical place where everyone has a butler and get my American dream.

What happened, though, was far from the dreamy life portrayed in The Fresh Prince of Bel-Air! When I was about to finish college, I was laid off from my company when it was shut down, and I was tired of the corporate world. I was an accountant who was overworked and hated going to my job every day. So, I decided to change my life by taking the risk and starting my own hair extension business.

I remember the visit that changed everything and put my life on a totally different trajectory! I had just gotten engaged to the love of my life and because the wedding day was fast approaching, I went to the beauty supply excited to get some hair extensions for my wedding day.

This visit was pretty much the same as all of my other visits to these stores – no one wanted to help me and I was followed around like I was going to steal something. I went from being super excited at finding the 'look' for my wedding day to feeling super uncomfortable and I started to just cry out of frustration and also anger. I was just tired of being treated so badly and I left the store without buying anything.

I immediately called my cousin and told her about my experience, and she said, "Girl, that is how it is! It happens to me more times than I care to remember!"

At first, I was outraged, and then I said to myself, "We

need better options than this! We need to be treated with respect at the places where we choose to spend our money!"

And that's how I decided to start a hair extension business that would have high-quality hair extensions and at the same time treat my customers with respect and gratitude.

I never imagined that it would grow into a 7 figure per year business! But I have done it and I believe that you can too!

I have learned a lot and also failed a lot since I started in 2007. I almost gave up trying to start my business after 18 months of struggling to find high-quality hair to sell. I lost over $50,000 buying from bad hair suppliers – every penny I had was gone.

As a last resort, I sold my own furniture! With that, I spent 3 months traveling all over the world trying to find the best quality hair that I could.

Yes, I struggled and failed on my way to having a successful hair business! Since then, I have made over $10,000,000 selling hair extensions online and I have helped over 6,000 students start their own online businesses. My business can fully support my lifestyle. I have the freedom to spend time with my two children, travel, and give back to my community.

Why I Wrote This Book

I am a strong believer in giving back. When I first began my business I told myself that if I became successful I would give back. Once my business had become successful, I decided to help fund a dialysis clinic in Kenya. One of my biggest passions is helping the children at the local orphanage by paying their school fees and providing day-to-day necessities such as food, toiletries, and school supplies.

When I started my business I had no clientele and I had no idea what to even say to potential customers. My wish is for you to shorten your learning curve and succeed much faster than I did by reading this book and learning some actionable hair business fundamentals.

People often ask me why I am so willing to share my secrets and help other people succeed in the industry that I am succeeding in. My first reason for this is that I am a giving person who believes in abundance. My second reason is that the hair extension industry is an $8 billion per year industry – there is space for everyone, and I believe that we can all succeed together.

Another reason why I am writing this book and sharing my knowledge is, "Why not us?"

Before I started my hair business, I had to endure lots of bad customer service experiences and bad quality hair. We spend over $8 billion a year on hair extensions – so why not also be a part of the money-making part of it?

I believe that if we spend money on our community, it goes back to our community, and the circle goes on and on.

What You Will Get From This Book

My goal is to motivate, inspire, and enable you to start your own hair extension business by sharing with you the untold secrets of starting a successful business. I have done all the research and learned lessons the hard way – now you can learn these lessons the easy way by reading this book and implementing them.

This book will empower you to start your own business without spending tens of thousands of dollars and without having to go through a dozen vendors before finding the right one.

The best part is you can do this even if you don't have an existing clientele – when I started out, I had never sold hair before and I had no idea what to do or say!

They say experience is the best teacher so by reading this book, you will be able to shorten your learning curve and perhaps even succeed faster than I did by applying my experience and lessons learned from running a hair business since 2007.

I have three assumptions as to why you are reading this book:

1. You are excited to have a hair business that can replace your current job, that also helps you earn more money and provide a high-quality service to your community at the same time.
2. You would like to be your own boss and make

money selling hair extensions.

3. You are looking for an additional income stream or side hustle.

In this book, I am going to show you:

1. The history and the future of the hair extension industry.
2. How to find a reliable and reputable vendor.
3. Which products to sell and pricing strategies.
4. How to maximize your hair sales.
5. How to make your brand stand out.
6. How to elevate your customer experience.
7. Mistakes to avoid.
8. Mindset hacks to build your own successful hair business.
9. Creative ways to fund your hair business.
10. What to do next to start your business today.

Full Disclosure

This is *not* a get-rich-quick scheme. During my journey into the hair extension industry, I lost so much money through scams and get-rich-quick schemes, and I do not want you to make the same mistake. This book does not promise you that you will create a successful business – I do not know your work ethic or history, and I cannot guarantee you anything. Even though this book will provide you with all of my tips and tricks, you will still need to put in the time, energy, dedication, and attention to make your business successful.

CHAPTER 1: THE HAIR EXTENSIONS INDUSTRY EXPLAINED

"I had to make my own living and my own opportunity. But I made it! Don't sit down and wait for the opportunities to come. Get up and make them."
— Madam C.J. Walker

The History Of Hair Extensions

Since I am writing about selling hair extensions, I thought it would be fun to start by talking about the exciting and remarkable history of extensions. I am sure that you will find this history amazing, and it will inspire you to be a part of the future of hair extensions. Hair extensions have come a long way since they were first used. New materials have been discovered over time and around the world that make higher-quality hair extensions, all the way up until what we have now. And who knows, maybe in the next few years we will find even better ways to source and take care of hair extensions!

So, to start with the history of hair extensions, we will look at the first documented use of hair extensions that came from the Ancient Egyptians, over 5,000 years ago! They placed and fixed wigs onto their heads and they also used sewn-on hairpieces and braids. These extensions were made from materials including human hair and dyed sheep wool, and to attach the extensions, resin and beeswax were used. These extensions were often black in color but there were also extensions made in blue, red, and gold. How cool is that?

Hair extensions in Egypt became popular again during Cleopatra's time – her favorite colored extension was peacock blue, and they made her look gorgeous!

Powdered wigs were also being used by males (yes, males!) and female royalties in Europe. These wigs were an indicator of wealth and status, and they projected power and health (they were especially used to hide any balding!).

For centuries, traditional African hair-braiding techniques have included extensions of some kind. These beautiful African hair extensions were decorated with items such as cowrie shells and feathers, making beautiful traditional hairstyles.

Now we move on to the noblewomen of the 1700s who had large, beehive-shaped weaves that were made of horsehair and wool frames. These weaves were woven into the woman's natural hair and made some stunning weaves!

Crazy fact you need to know – hair extensions were only for the upper classes until the early 20th century. This changed because the use of hairpins created an opportunity for the average woman to experiment with big, beautiful hair. Hats and hairpins helped to create volume and lift curls, creating the illusion of fuller hair. Women also started collecting hairs caught in their hair brushes and used them to add volume to the hair on their head!

Then in the 60s, clip-in hair extensions started being made and became a common trend, along with beehive-style hairpieces.

In the 70s, the Pompadour look had become the latest trend, and to create this look women had to use hair extensions and frames. This caused a huge increase in demand for hair extensions and is possibly the groundbreaking trend that has led to the mass production of hair extensions today! This was a very exciting time for the hair extension industry, and we should remember this time period because it helped us get to where we are now in the hair industry.

If we look at the 80s, hair extensions had become commonplace and African American weaves were being made in many different styles that women could create!

The 90s were all about the clip-ins and hair of any color, and many styles became available. This made it a fun time for experimenting!

Today, hair extension technology means we can get 'virgin hair' extensions – hair extensions made of real hair that has never been colored or treated! This is the type of hair that we at WealthyHair.com use. Hair extensions are also used by people with hair loss, African Americans, Orthodox Jewish, celebrities, and, really, anyone who is looking for longer hair or more volume.

There seems to be endless possibilities when it comes to the development of high-quality, beautiful hair extensions, and the future for hair extensions is very exciting. So I hope that you are excited to become part of the history of hair extensions!

Where Hair Extensions Come From

To sell high-quality hair, you need to know where it comes from and the best places to get it from. I traveled the world for 3 months to find where the best hair is found! I will share with you where this hair comes from and what types of hair you can find.

High-quality virgin hair is sourced from many different places in many different ways. The process that I describe below is the best way to source hair today and is how we at Wealthy Hair get our hair extensions, after spending years perfecting the virgin hair process to optimize quality and also the ability for the hair to have minimal to no shedding plus last a long time.

The process of where hair comes from starts with harvesting. Basically, this is the collection of the hair from someone's head. The majority of unprocessed hair comes from India and Myanmar. Other sources include local hair traders in China and India who search for women who are willing to sell their long locks.

In most cases, hair needs to be at least 10 inches long to be sellable, this is about 2 years of growing your hair. The price of the hair varies depending on its length, texture and condition, but don't worry, I will show you which hair is best and which hair you should buy to sell so that you do not spend any more money than you need to, to start selling hair extensions.

Hair cut directly from the head gets you the highest price, earning its nickname, 'black gold.'

In Southern India's Hindu temples, pilgrims sacrifice their hair in a practice called tonsuring.

Tonsure is the practice of cutting or shaving some or all of the hair on the scalp as a sign of religious devotion or humility. Tonsure is a major source of unprocessed or virgin hair.

For example, in Venkateswara Temple, Tirumala, around 1,300 barbers shave an average of 40 heads each per day. This hair is then sold through e-auctions. In 2019, one of these auctions sold for $1.6 million for a 157 tons of hair! This shows just how big the hair market is, and how much potential there is for you to join it.

As communities develop and become more modern, women are becoming less willing to sell their hair. This has forced harvesters in India and China to look for hair in other places such as Indonesia, Mongolia, Myanmar, and Laos. The good news is these hair origins still offer you great-quality hair that you would be proud to sell to your customers.

In 2018 in Yangon, Myanmar, hairdressers were offering between $11 and $150 for a head of hair! This amount of money is a lot compared to the normal income people make from their working wages of an average of about $300 per month in that country.

Unfortunately, due to an unbalanced level of supply and demand, the industry also relies on less desirable hair – waste hair. This is the hair that the hair pickers gather from drains, salon floors, and other waste, and sell to local dealers (gross!). I have learned the hard way about buying this hair and discovering how poor the quality of this hair is. I wasted so much money buying this cheaper hair thinking that I could buy huge quantities, but just like with everything else in life, you get what you pay for! Plus it is hard to get repeat customers.

This is one of the reasons I decided to focus on quality vs cheap and I refused to ever buy waste hair ever again.

This waste hair goes to Myanmar and Bangladesh where it is untangled and sorted into bundles of matching length and color. This hair is definitely not what you want to sell to customers and we at Wealthy Hair do not buy this hair. You want to provide your customers with high-quality, beautiful hair, not waste! In a later chapter, I will show you how to tell whether the hair is real hair or if it is synthetic, so keep reading if you want to hear more about this!

Once harvesting has been completed, the clumps of hair are processed into organized manes. This processed hair is shipped to factories. There, it is manufactured into clip-in bangs, bobs, and toupees. The hair is dyed, treated, hand-knotted, and machine-wefted into custom wigs that are handmade on molds of heads.

The final step of hair extension creation, before it is sent to stores, is sanitization. Some raw virgin hair has nits and you, of course, want these removed. This is done by removing them by hand using gentle cleansers. At Wealthy Hair, we use apple cider vinegar and gentle shampoos to do this. Always be sure to ask your supplier what their sanitization process is.

The finished product is then shipped to salons and other retailers of hair extensions along a global distribution chain. These products are shipped through multinational distributors and local sellers.

Fun Fact: Did you know that the United States is the largest buyer of human hair products? So there is so much potential to start your hair extension business immediately.

A significant portion of this final product goes to the African American market that is dominated by Korean American retailers. The market for sheitels (high-end wigs worn by Orthodox Jewish wives) also takes up a significant share of the U.S. market. A new U.S. market for hair extensions is currently being born and raised – millennials who use hair extensions for beauty on social media.

Unfortunately, most consumers do not know where their hair comes from, and it is often just assumed that the hair is sourced cleanly and ethically, but as we saw with waste hair, there are some sources of hair that are unethical. Some of these suppliers are known to supplement '100% human' hair with cheap synthetic materials or animal hair or misrepresent the origin of the hair, so always make sure that your supplier is trustworthy, reliable, and honest about where they source their hair. I have seen the different types of hair and Wealthy Hair only provides the highest-quality virgin hair and this is one of the reasons we have been able to last in the hair industry for a long time!

As to where the future of hair extensions is going, Raw Society Hair has now developed hair extensions made from banana tree stems. The goal of this is to help reduce unethically (or grossly) sourced hair being sold. This means that the hair extension industry is growing and becoming better and better every year and that there is space for you in this industry!

The goal for any successful hair extension business should be to sell high-quality, reliably sourced hair extensions that have gone through harvesting, fabrication, and sanitization. Once the hair has been shipped to sellers, they can begin selling it!

So now that you know where hair extensions come from, I am positive you now have the information you need to find a reliable hair vendor that provides you with consistent quality hair to keep your customers coming back over and over again.

The Statistics Of The Hair Extension Industry

The statistics of the hair extension industry will amaze you and make you excited to be in this growing industry. When I entered this industry, I was completely new to it. I had not worked in any hair business and I was not in the selling industry. I started right from the bottom and I was able to build a million-dollar business because of the way that the hair extension industry is moving.

$8 billion (with a B!) worth of hair extensions are sold every year in the USA alone! And according to UN Comtrade data, China exported $1.15 billion worth of manufactured human hair products in 2019! With more than $130 million worth of 2020 imports, the United States is the largest market for hair extensions. How exciting are these numbers? This is a huge industry!

Looking into the future, there is an obvious growth in the hair industry and the statistics over the past few years prove this. Hair extension usage in the USA has increased 35% to 50% every year since 2004, that is huge! This increase is expected to grow even more over the next few years, so if you are looking to join the hair extension industry, now is the perfect time to do it!

But with such a big market, how will you stand out against competition that is already in the industry? That is what this book is all about! I have learned where the gaps in this market are and I am sharing that with you now. You have the opportunity to take advantage of what is missing in the industry right now: there is poor customer service at beauty supply shops that you can improve on that is guaranteed to make customers return to your business rather than go to shops where they are treated poorly, and the poor quality of hair extensions out there provides you with a gap to fill with high-quality hair extensions that will make customers never want to buy poor-quality hair again!

The opportunities in the hair extension industry are huge and are growing every year, so you really can do it. I am just a normal person who decided to make my own business, and I was able to make it successful, so you can do this too!

The Future And Growth Of The Hair Extensions Industry

As I said before, hair extension usage in the USA is increasing by 35% to 50% *every year*. This shows incredible potential for the industry, which is projected to increase from $8 billion per year to $10 billion per year by 2024! And with my help, you can make your business more successful because you will start your business without making any mistakes!

Even during the COVID-19 pandemic, the hair extension business continued to flourish. During times in 2020 when salons and beauty shops were closed, sales of health and beauty products rose by 13% compared to the same months of 2019. This is because customers tend to spend more on small indulgences (such as hair extensions) during tough financial times. How exciting is it to be part of an industry that can survive, and even flourish, during difficult times?

In addition to this, studies have been showing that customers have started viewing salon expenses such as hair extensions as essentials rather than luxuries. This means that more customers will be purchasing hair extensions more frequently and regularly, further growing the industry!

I am so excited to share this industry with you because with so much potential, the hair industry is going to grow and grow and it has a very bright future that I am sure you would love to be a part of.

CHAPTER 2: HOW TO FIND A RELIABLE VENDOR

> *"Knowledge is Power, Power provides Information; Information leads to Education, Education breeds Wisdom; Wisdom is Liberation. People are not liberated because of lack of knowledge."*
> — *Israelmore Ayivor*

Qualities Of A Good Vendor

I have to tell you, having a good vendor is a lesson I learned the hard way. You see, in the beginning before I became a hair vendor, I had no one to show me the way and that is why it was very important that I had a super detailed guide on how to find a good vendor. As I am sure you are aware, the quality of your vendor determines the quality of the products that you sell. So here are the things that you should look out for when you are choosing a vendor.

A good vendor offers 4 qualities that you should look out for:

1. Good communication: You want a vendor who communicates well, responds to your inquiries, and is available in emergencies. You don't want a vendor who you cannot contact or who is unreliable when you need them. Always judge a vendor by how they treat you before you buy. Are they responsive? If someone treats you badly before you buy from them, they will actually treat you horribly after you give them your money.

2. Time in the business: A vendor who has been in the industry for a long time and that is accredited can be more trusted for good service and products. I have learned that you want a vendor who has been in the business for at least five to ten years.

3. Specialty: If the vendor does not focus on hair-related products only and sells everything such as phone cases, yoga pants, bedsheets, etc, then they are probably not producing the highest-quality hair and are most likely middlemen. Do your research on the vendor and make sure that they have hair extensions as their priority.

4. Reliability: You want a vendor that you can rely on for good quality and for express delivery when required. In the beginning, I wasted so much money buying from vendors who were unreliable and did not keep their delivery promises. The last thing that we want is for a customer who is buying last-minute to not get what they need by the time that they need it.

A good hair vendor controls all of the three hair production processes in-house so that they can provide consistent quality. These three hair production processes include:

1. Harvesting

- How does your vendor get their hair and what type is it? I could have saved so much money by asking vendors this question.
- Ensure that all of the cuticles of the hair they provide are intact and are facing the same direction, you don't want to waste your money buying waste hair that will tangle when customers wash it or wear it.
- Be careful about waste hair – as I said before, waste hair is gathered from salon and barbershop floors, it's not high-quality! They strip the cuticles and coat the hair with silicon so that the hair looks nice, however once the hair is washed, it tangles.

2. Fabrication

- The vendor's wefting technique is important because it affects tangling, ease of installation, and shedding. Ask your vendor what they do to prevent these so that you don't waste time and money with a vendor who does not provide high-quality hair.
- Ensure that the vendors seal the weft – there must be no shedding and it must be run through the weft. Again, you want the best quality hair. At Wealthy Hair, we always seal the weft, then the hair extensions are wefted 3 times to ensure there is minimal shedding. We don't want our clients to be always sweeping their

bathroom floor because their hair extensions are shedding too much. No one, including me, has time for that!

- Your clients obviously want to use their hair, so they will need to have it installed! You want to make sure that the weft is not very thick so that it is easy for the needle to go through when the client is getting the install done.

3. Sanitization

- Raw hair might have nits, and you of course want to make sure that your supplier removes them.
- The best way to remove nits is *by hand.* Although this is tedious, this is one of the things we do at Wealthy Hair as it is necessary to keep the integrity of the hair.
- I have to warn you that some vendors try to 'cheat' this tedious process and may use harsh chemicals such as insecticides or detergents that are bad for you and may even cause an itchy scalp. These chemicals also make it difficult to keep the cuticles intact. So ensure your vendor does not use these chemicals.

Another aspect of ensuring your vendor is a good one is to examine the cuticles of the hair they provide. The cuticle of the hair is the lifeline of the hair extensions. If the cuticles are all intact and facing the same direction the result will be durable, shiny, and real-looking hair.

You can take a quick video tour of the Wealthy Hair factory here: WealthyHair.com/Factory and it will show you what the process of creating hair extensions and ensuring what excellent quality looks like. This process has come from experience gained over 15 years of research and trial and error.

Below are some of our processes to ensure that our hair is of the highest quality for our clients:

- First, the hair is sealed to ensure that it has minimal to no shedding.
- The hair is run through a waft three times. If any hair falls it is not picked up. We make sure that the cuticles are facing the same direction in this process (this helps the hair to not tangle). This ensures a strong waft and prevents shedding when the hair is brushed.
- Any loose hairs are removed.
- The hair is steam (not chemically) processed to ensure that the hair quality is protected.
- The quality assurance team then goes through every single pack of hair making sure that each bundle of hair that is sold is of outstanding quality before it goes to a customer.

Questions To Ask A Potential Vendor

Guys, it is important to get to know a vendor before you decide to commit to them. It is extremely important that your vendor provides you with the best possible hair so that you can sell the best hair on the market – this will make customers come back to you every time they need hair extensions.

After being in the hair industry for over 15 years, I have

summarized the most important questions that you need to ask your hair vendor.

Here are 20 questions to ask potential vendors that will help you learn more about them and their standard of hair quality.

1. Where do you get your hair from? Find out whether your vendor gets real virgin hair or if they collect waste hair and treat it with chemicals.
2. What type of hair do you collect? Ponytail hair is the best option for high-quality virgin hair.
3. Can you describe your wefting technique step by step? This will show you how committed the vendor is to creating high-quality hair.
4. What do you do to prevent tangling? Find out what techniques the vendor uses to ensure the hair does not tangle.
5. How do you ensure that your hair is easy to install? The weft cannot be too thick as the needle needs to penetrate it during the sew-in process. What do you do to prevent shedding? Find out if your vendor does anything specific to prevent the hair from shedding.
6. Do you seal the weft? Make sure that your vendor seals the weft for high-quality and durable hair.
7. Do you remove nits from your hair? This is important – you don't want a client finding nits in their hair! What is your process for removing nits? By hand is the preferred method.
8. Do you use any chemicals on your hair? At Wealthy Hair, we only use a steam process to protect the

integrity and not alter the chemical composition of the hair. No perms or relaxers.

9. What quality control processes do you use? Quality control ensures that customers only receive high-quality goods.

10. How do you ensure that the cuticles of the hair are in good condition? The cuticles are the lifeline of the hair and you want them to be in the best condition possible.

11. How quickly can you be contacted? In case of an emergency, you want to be able to call them on the phone and get quick answers from them.

12. Are you accredited or rated by the Better Business Bureau? This is a sign of good reliability and trustworthiness.

13. Do you only sell hair-related products? You want a vendor who is focused on hair and not putting their efforts into other products such as make-up and handbags.

14. How long have you been in the business? At least 5-10 years is ideal.

15. Do you have any referrals and reviews? These will help you see how satisfied or unsatisfied the vendor's previous clients have been with the quality of their hair.

16. Are you able to do same-day shipping? Clients will love it if you can offer them fast delivery, especially if they are ordering last minute.

17. Do you have overnight delivery? Fast delivery times will give you an advantage over competitors who cannot offer this.

18. Do you offer better rates for slower delivery? If an order is not rushed, a client may be happier to pay less for delivery.
19. What do you charge for delivery? Ensure that it makes economic sense to use their delivery services – you will have to factor in this cost.
20. What are your expectations from our side? Find out what they expect from you – upfront payments, bulk orders, etc.

Choosing a reliable hair vendor is a must if you want to have a long-lasting hair business. The only reason WealthyHair.com has been able to last this long in the hair industry is because we have made quality the biggest priority. If you offer your customers high-quality hair, they will come back over and over again. This means you can create recurring income with your business and have the freedom of time and money. This also means you don't have to hustle for your next dollar every single day.

How To Test Hair Quality

I have been asked numerous times for my advice on how to test the quality of hair your hair vendor is sending you.

One of the best ways to do this is to look at reviews from previous customers and you will also be able to judge from how the hair vendor answers your questions (from the previous page).

Here are more tips for buying hair from vendors that I

have learned over the years:

- Pay using trusted methods such as PayPal or credit card and make sure that you get receipts – this will ensure that you do not get scammed out of money.
- Be careful when choosing vendors based on price. You get what you pay for and because of its demand, raw hair has become expensive. Buy hair based on its qualities rather than its price, trust me on this one. In the long run, you will see how important this is.
- Buy from vendors in the same country as you when you are starting out.

Below are some ways to test the hair if you deem it necessary:

The Burn Test

This first test will help you determine whether the hair is human or synthetic. The test compares what happens to virgin remy hair versus synthetic or mixed blend hair when you burn them. Virgin hair means that it is not dyed or chemically processed in any way, and remy means that the cuticles are intact and facing the same direction and that it is virgin hair. Mixed blend hair is hair that is natural but has been through chemical processing. Most hair that is available at beauty supply stores is synthetic or mixed. To do the experiment, you will need a bunch of the hair that you want to test and a lighter. Take the hair and carefully burn the hair. Let the hair cool down for a few minutes then assess it:

- Virgin hair will burn into a dark grey ash, and the burning will smell similar to how it smells when you flat iron your hair.
- Synthetic hair does not turn into ash – it becomes more of a hardball, and it smells like burnt plastic.

The Color Test

The coloring test helps you determine the quality of the hair. If the hair quality is good, it should be able to go from its natural black color to Hair Color #613 (Bleach Blonde).

The Shedding Test

A good manufacturer will always seal the hair before making it into a weft. Run your hands through the hair – there should only be minimal shedding.

So, there you go. These are all of my tips and tricks that I have been learning since 2007 to make sure that the quality of the hair from vendors is impeccable and that the hair is 100% natural. Be sure to use these on all hair samples and bulk orders from vendors to make sure that you are selling only high-quality hair that your customers will come back for.

Here is the link to the video showing you how to test for the hair quality: WealthyHair.com/HairTest

How To Avoid Being Scammed By Vendors

When I first started out in 2007, I was swindled a few times by vendors, and I lost a lot of money and time to these scams. I don't want you to get scammed as I did, so here is my story on how I was scammed by a vendor:

After doing my research and finally finding a vendor I liked, I ordered a small sample of their hair to test it out and see its quality, and loved the quality of the hair! I was so excited that I had found this vendor with such great hair that I made a big order from them, but when the big order arrived I was so disappointed. The quality of this hair was terrible compared to the samples! This almost put me out of the hair extension business entirely. So, my advice for you to avoid this scam is to gradually increase your order size each time you order from them and make sure that the quality of the hair in each order is acceptable. Once you reach a large order size and are still happy with the hair, then go for it and keep ordering from that vendor! But if the quality decreases when you start making larger orders, then stop ordering from that vendor and find a new one.

So, be careful with scams like this one, use my advice and experience of this to make sure that you don't learn about these scams the hard way.

CHAPTER 3: CHOOSING THE RIGHT PRODUCTS TO SELL & PRICING STRATEGIES

"Embrace what you don't know, especially in the beginning, because what you don't know can become your greatest asset. It ensures that you will absolutely be doing things different from everybody else."
— Sara Blakely

Types Of Hair Extensions

One of the most exciting parts of the hair extension industry is the number of different types of hair extensions. There is such a variety of hair extensions, different styles, lengths, and pieces – it might be a bit overwhelming! But don't worry, I am going to explain all of these different styles so you have a deeper understanding on how to best serve your customers.

Hair weft extensions are a collection of hair strands that have been sewn into a thin strip that is ready to be installed into your hair. Hair wefts can be machine sewn or hand sewn.

Clip-in hair extensions are an easy, fast, and safe way to get long, thick hair. Clip-in hair extension wefts come with clips attached to them that you simply clip into your hair. You can do this yourself, without the need for a salon professional, and get beautiful thick, long hair that you can take out whenever you want. If you take good care of your hair extensions, they can last up to 12 months, but usually, they last 3 to 6 months, at which point you will need to buy new ones to replace them.

Hot fusion hair extensions require the help of a salon professional. The extensions are attached by the salon professional by attaching strands of hair onto the client's head with a keratin-based tip. A heating element is used to attach the keratin bond and extension to the hair. This method of hair extension will not damage your hair, is comfortable, and will last 3 to 5 months.

Tape-in extensions are one-inch wide wefts that are pre-taped, made of a medical-grade adhesive. This adhesive is used to attach the wefts to your hair.

Lace frontals are the current trend. They are used to recreate the front hairline from ear to ear. They are often 4 inches to the back and 13 inches across, helping to complete your hair extension look. They are versatile and look flawless – as if the hair is growing from your real scalp. Lace frontals can be sew-in or bonded with glue or tape installations. Lace frontals allow you to try different hairstyles such as different partings or ponytails that look natural. Lace frontals have a low installation time of about 1 hour.

Lace closures are used to recreate the natural parting of the hairline. They typically come in 4x4 inch size and are used to close off a style. They are available in different styles: 3-part closures allow you to part the hair in 3 different ways; middle part closures allow you to part the hair in the middle; free part closures let you part your hair however you wish and is, therefore, the most versatile option. Lace closures require little maintenance, last longer than lace frontals, and protect your hair.

A wig is an artificial head covering made from hair (real hair, animal hair, or synthetic fibers). This can be styled and colored as you want and is an alternative to extensions. Wigs are better for people with conditions such as hair loss, thin hair, or damaged hair, where hair extensions are impossible or will further damage hair.

What To Consider When Starting Out

When I started out, I was completely new to the hair extensions industry and I did not know what products to sell, so I wasted a lot of time and money testing and trying to figure out what products would actually sell. Feel free to use this as a guide especially when you are starting out, keep in mind you can always expand and add more products as your business grows.

I suggest that you start with selling what I have found to be the most popular products. I have tested out over 50 products, and nothing outsells virgin hair weave extensions, so this is where you should start. After lots of testing along with lots of trial and error selling anything from 8" to 36" hair lengths, I have found the products that sell the best:

- The best-selling hair lengths are 12" to 20".
- The best hair quality type is pure virgin human hair extensions.
- The most popular hairstyle is wavy hair – it is versatile, low maintenance, and looks beautiful, so invest your money here.
- The best-selling age demographics are 31-year-olds to 50-year-olds – so focus your attention here.

When it comes to inventory when you first start out, it is important to invest properly in the best and most popular selling products. I have lost a lot of money by stocking the wrong things and I don't want you to make the same mistakes. So here is some advice:

- Weaves:
  - Stock at least lengths of 12" to 24".
  - The textures that sell the best are body wave, curly, straight, and yaki straight.
- Closures and frontals:
  - Stock lace frontals and lace closures from 12-16" in straight, wavy, curly, and relaxed yaki straight.
  - You need to stock at least 10 of each length.
  - Stock in virgin Brazilian, Indian, Malaysian, and Peruvian.

As you get more customers, you can do something that

I have learned that has helped my company grow: ask for feedback to see what else they would like to buy and slowly add those products as your company grows. But I would strongly recommend to NOT try to be everything to everyone... This was another lesson I had to learn the hard way. You will want to make sure you have a real demand of a particular product. Like if you have multiple customers continually asking for a product to sell that is when you would consider adding it. Don't try to add anything and everything customers ask for because that will just make your inventory costs go through the roof and you could just be stuck with products that very rarely sell.

Repeat business is what adds a lot to your company – you want the same customers to come back to you over and over again, so their opinion is important. Also remember that your customers are your walking billboards. If they are walking around with beautiful hair that they are happy with, they will recommend your business to their friends, which will get you more customers, more business, and more profit.

I have 3 other super tips that I have learned along the way and that have helped me have a million dollar hair business:

Profit Maximizer Tip 1: When your customers are checking out, ask them if they would like to add on a closure or frontal to their order. This has added so much to my profits and it will add to yours too. Prompting your customer to buy extra pieces that will make their hair extensions look even more beautiful will easily increase your monthly revenue by 30% to 40%.

Profit Maximizer Tip 2: This is another profit maximizer that really gets you to close sales. I always offer bundle deals. The bundles of hair extensions are sold for slightly cheaper than what they would cost to buy each item individually. You can also bundle hair extensions with closures or frontals to offer the client a full look in one purchase.

This makes it easier for the customer to shop with you, which increases the chances of them buying from you again. You usually need 3 packs of hair for a sew-in, and the best-selling bundles that I have found are packs of 12" + 14" + 16" and packs of 14" + 16" + 18". The more bundles like this that a customer buys, the more money you will make.

Profit Maximizer Tip 3: Gain trust by assuring the customer that if they don't use the hair, they can return it within 30 days and get a refund. I can tell you that this will help you convert so many website visitors into customers because this will make the customer feel more at ease when buying your hair, and more likely to buy from you than another seller who does not offer a return policy. This can help customers who are on the fence about whether they want to buy from you or not. Do not worry about whether you will lose money, because if the hair that you send to your customer is of high quality, they are likely to use it and keep it – only around 1% of customers will return their products.

Pricing Strategies

I have been selling hair since 2007 – that's a long time! Over that time, I have done a lot of trial and error, research, and gained first-hand experience to perfect my pricing strategies. It is so important because if your pricing strategy is not solid, you may end up losing money instead! So, here is my advice on what to consider when creating yours:

1. **Cost to acquire the customer:** This is how much it costs your business to acquire a customer. Below are some costs to consider.

2. **Employee costs:** Trust me, when you start getting lots of customers, it is going to be difficult to run your business on your own. At $10/hour, 1 employee will cost $20,000 a year. You will likely need at least some employees to ensure fast delivery of purchases, and excellent customer service, so you need to consider how many employees you need to help you run the business smoothly, what you are willing to pay those employees, and how that will affect your profits.

3. **Advertising:** Hopefully, your satisfied customers will act as walking billboards for your company. If your customers have great hair, they will want to show it off and they will tell everyone where they got their hair from. This will bring in customers for you because they will also want such gorgeous hair. But if you want to have more advertising than that, you will need to pay for it. Social media ads all cost

money, and the more advertising you want to do to grow, the more it is going to cost. So consider how much advertising will cost and how that cost will affect your profits (it could increase your profits if it leads to more sales, or decrease profits if it does not).

4. **Rent:** If you plan on having a store front, then you will need to pay rent and utilities. Consider these expenses when pricing your products. But I would recommend focusing on selling everything online instead of a store front just because of the very large expenses incurred from opening and maintaining a physical store. (Another one of those things I had learned the hard way)

5. **Shipping costs:** You will need to pay your supplier to ship their products to you and you need to pay for shipping when you ship to your customers.

6. **What market are you going after?** Think Louis Vuitton vs Walmart.

   a. Do you want a high-end business that focuses on one category type of products and offers the best quality products that your customers will find in the market? In this case, you can price your products slightly higher.

   b. Do you want a mass-market business that offers a large number of different categories of products at a lower cost, but will bring in more customers due to its affordability and access to other products on your site? Then you will have to have slightly lower prices (and profit margins).

7. **Your income goals:**

   a. If you are selling high-quality products, you can expect to make $30-$50 profit per pack of hair and most customers buy 3 packs. This means that for the average customer, your profit could be an average of $90 or more.

   b. **Here is a success tip**: Start with the end in mind. It is important you break down your goals so that you know exactly what to achieve.

   c. If you need to make a $3,000 profit per month and each pack is $30 profit, that means you need to sell 100 bundles or get about 33 customers, which means you need to sell to 1 customer per day.

   d. This table shows you how many packs you need to sell to how many customers in order to make your income goal for the month. Start with a small goal, such as $3,000, and work your way up to getting an average of 9 customers per day, where you will be making $25,000 a month!

Income goal for the month	Packs need to sell per month	# of customers needed per month – most customers buy 3 packs	Customers needed per day
$3,000	100	33	1
$5,000	166	55	1-2 customers per day
$10,000	332	110	3-4 customers per day
$25,000	833	277	9 customers per day

I know I have given you a lot of information and I would like to assure you that it is not as overwhelming or hard to implement as it may seem. I believe in working smarter not harder and that is why I have a free masterclass on the quickest and simplest way to launch your hair business. Visit this link for more information:

WealthyHair.com/Webinar

Some tips on pricing your hair extensions

When I started in this industry, I had no idea how to price any of my products. I had to do a lot of research and test different prices for each of my products until I found the perfect prices. Your business is unique to you, so I cannot tell you exactly how to price your products, but I can give you some advice:

a. Start with higher prices and offer new customers coupons or 'opening specials' so that you can see what customers are willing to pay. This also gives your customers an opportunity to pay 'special prices' so that they can try out your product and find out that they love it, and they will be more willing to pay more for it when they no longer have the discount.

b. I see a lot of new hair business owners who think that if they lower the price of their hair extensions, the more business they will get. Using pricing as your only competitive advantage is a quick race to the bottom and you will not last in the industry for a long time. There is always someone willing to sell for less!

c. It may take some tests and trials to see what customers are willing to pay, but if you offer them high-quality products and fantastic customer service, they will come back to you even if they have to pay more for it.

d. Offering regular specials and coupons will also bring returning and new customers to you frequently and help you see how much more traffic you can bring in by lowering your prices slightly. Sales work, this is why 99% of every company out there runs them!

It took me a while to get all of my pricing strategies just right, so it may take you a while too, but with my advice, you will be able to get yours perfected much sooner than I did. You want to be smart about your pricing strategies. It is more important to know what inventory you should start with – you do not want to buy inventory from your vendor and lose money because nobody wants to buy it! I have provided you with my knowledge on what each hair product is and which products sell the best so that you do not make the same mistakes that I did.

It is important to make sure that once you have paid for all of your start-up expenses and your monthly expenses, you will be making a profit once your business is up and running. Having a strong pricing strategy makes sure that you will be making the most possible money from your customers and that you are taking home a profit every month. Finding the best possible pricing strategy for your company may take some trial and error, but once you have perfected it you will be maximizing your sales, your profit, your returning customers, bringing in new customers, and running a successful business.

Also, I highly recommend that you attend my masterclass where I will show you exactly how to start your business with as few start-up costs as possible, and how to keep your company running with as few expenses as possible. Sign up here to attend my masterclass:

WealthyHair.com/Webinar

CHAPTER 4: MAXIMIZING YOUR HAIR SALES

> *The road to success and greatness is always paved with consistent hard work. Outwork your competitors, be authentic, and above all else, chase your greatness."*
> — *Dwayne 'The Rock' Johnson*

Creating Hair Bundles

I know that I have talked briefly about this, but it is worth repeating because creating hair bundles is a great way to make more money per purchase. It has increased my profits tremendously. This is an excellent profit maximizer that I have learned over the years. When you offer hair bundles, you make it easier for customers to find all of the products that they need in one purchase. This will increase not only the chances of your customer buying from you because of the convenience, but you will also make more money when you sell bundles compared to selling individual pieces. Customers will also love it if you offer your bundles at a discount compared to buying the individual pieces. Everyone loves savings and offering discounts for bundle deals will be a big incentive for your customers to buy larger quantities.

Over the years, I have learned that the best thing is to offer your bundle deals according to the different styles and hair types that you have available. Each style (Body Wavy Hair Weave, Island Curly Hair Weave, Natural Straight Hair Weave, Yaki Relaxed Straight Hair Weave) should have bundle deals. As a reference, remember that the most popular bundle lengths are the combinations of 12" + 14" + 16" and combinations of 14" + 16" + 18".

Building An Email List

Building an email list is crucial and also an easy way to get repeat customers. In my experience, I have found this to be a great marketing tool that is a very low cost thing to do and my biggest asset. Also remember to get consent to send promotions when customers provide their email when they make an order on your website. This can easily be done by your website programmer on the checkout page. You can also create a banner on your website that offers customers a discount on their first purchase if they sign up to your email list. Research shows that about 10% or more is a good incentive for someone to give you their email address. This will encourage customers to not only make their first purchase with you, but they will also now receive content and promotional emails from you.

It is important that you keep your email list engaged. I

usually make sure to send an email to my list at least once a week. If you are starting out, you can start with at least every other week if you prefer. Apart from sending promotional emails, make sure you send out helpful content such as how to take care of the hair extensions, as an example. By keeping in contact with your customers via email, you will be on top of their minds when it is time for them to buy new hair extensions.

Make sure to include direct links to your website on your marketing emails so that when customers open the email, they can click on the link to visit your website and shop.

Encourage Repeat Sales

The best way to create recurring income is to have repeat customers. Customers tend to come back to a business that has offered them great products at reasonable prices, those that have provided them with excellent customer service, and those businesses they can buy from conveniently and without hassle. So first, be sure to provide all of these things for your customers to ensure that they come back to you instead of looking elsewhere.

Most hair extension users will buy new extensions about every 3 months, and this provides an opportunity for hair extension businesses to make recurring income. Think about creating loyalty points for customers to encourage them to return to your store whenever they need new extensions. They can accumulate these points over a few sales and collect enough to earn a discount or coupon for a future purchase; this will encourage the customer back to your website/store to buy every time. Or, you can include a coupon code with every purchase that a customer makes to bring them back to your store/website for their next order.

Not only will your repeat customers bring in regular sales for you, but customers who repeatedly buy from you will also recommend you to their friends. With that in mind, offer them discounts to share with their friends and family. When you have repeat customers, make sure that you get to know them. It is important to get to know your customers, ask about their families and what is important in their lives. I have countless customers who will call to share happy news with me such as they are getting married or their kids graduated from college. They know that they matter as Wealthy Hair customers. When people feel valued, they will always stay loyal to you.

Also when your customers are shopping with you, you can ask more about why they are buying the hair. Perhaps it is for a special occasion or vacation? You can use this information to recommend the right products and also recommend more products to the client in the future, including new products that have just hit your virtual shelves!

Holiday Sales

Holidays are great times to generate extra sales because people are happy and celebrating and want to look good. Here are some holidays that generate a lot of sales for us, year in, year out:

- Valentine's Day
- New Year's Eve
- Halloween
- Thanksgiving
- 4th of July
- Mothers' Day

Two or three weeks before the dates such as the ones mentioned, start marketing (via emails, social media, etc.) that you are having a sale for that holiday. This will remind customers that a holiday is approaching and they need to get ready for it by getting a new hairstyle.

You can also ask customers to create an account with your business and add their birthday – then for their birthday month, you can offer them a birthday discount which will encourage them to buy from you in that month.

Offer An Upsell And Recommended Products

In my experience, I have learned that customers like convenience. They like to find everything in one place, and they want to find all of it quickly.

While you can make your business specialize in hair extensions, you can really increase your sales and customers by creating a site that offers more. If you sell shampoos, conditioners, oils, brushes, and hair accessories on your website, along with hair extensions, then you will become a one-stop-shop for everything that your customer will need for their hair. This makes it more convenient for your customer as they will only need to buy from your website to get everything they need for their hair.

As your company grows, you can expand on this even more and sell other beauty-related products such as make-up, handbags, accessories, eyelashes, and body creams. This will make your store a customer go-to when they are looking to create a complete look. Customers are also more likely to buy more from your brand if they know it and love it and can get everything they need from it.

Having this variety of items on your website/store adds to your brand and will increase your sales and return customers as they know it is the one place they need to go to get everything they need conveniently.

Selling all of these items also creates an excellent opportunity for bundle products – gift bundles! A husband who knows that his wife likes your brand but has no idea what she buys from it will be happy to find that you have gift bundles with hair products that he knows his wife will love! You can create bundles of hair products that go with hair extensions or a set of hair care products. Even your regular customers may buy these gift bundles for someone else who will then become a customer after testing your quality products.

Just remember that whatever it is that you sell on your website, it must still be really good quality! The most important thing is to always have good quality. This is what will get you repeat customers, new customers from word-of-mouth, and a really good reputation. So make sure that you are selling the best quality products that you can.

Follow Up With Prospective Customers

It is very common for most people to visit your website or store and not buy anything. It is part of having a business, so do not be disappointed by this. All you need to convert some of them into customers is to have a solid retargeting/follow-up strategy.

If someone visits your website and does not complete the checkout process, and leaves the cart with items, your website should be able to send them an email letting them know they forgot items in the cart.

Below is an example of an email they would get from WealthyHair.com

Re:[Insert Customer Name,] Did You Forget Something?

Hi gorgeous,

I just wanted to let you know that the items you added to the shopping cart are selling out quickly. What can I say? You have excellent taste 😜

I saved all the items you added to your cart for NOW. If you still want the items, please order now or **RISK COMPLETELY MISSING OUT.** ➡

CLICK HERE TO COMPLETE YOUR ORDER

We are serious about our 💯**% satisfaction guarantee!** If for any reason, you are not satisfied with your purchase, ship it back, and we will issue you a refund right away. Please note that the hair has to be new, unused, and in its original packaging (pretty fair, right?).

P.S.S. - Questions? Call us at 1-855-500-4321 or email us at Help@WealthyHair.com

COMPLETE MY ORDER

Thanks again for your support!

With Thanks,
Julia Strunk
President and Founder
WealthyHair.com

Sending cart abandonment emails is a great way to increase your customers. As you can see from the above email, not only does it communicate the scarcity so they can take action right away, it also handles a very common objection of what happens if they do not like the hair.

Below are some stats of how much I have made recently from the above email alone:

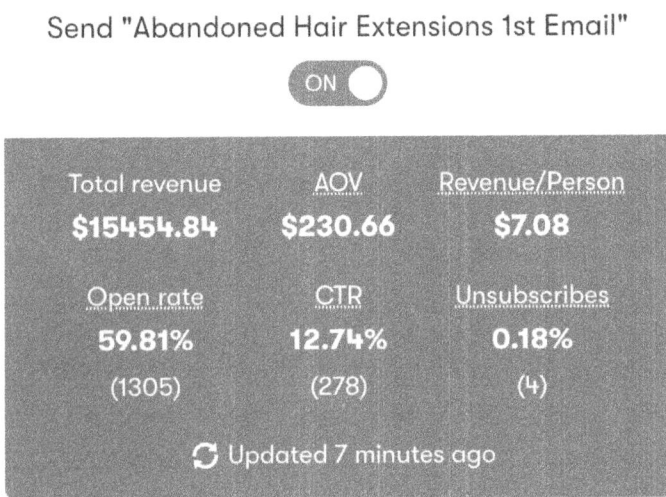

Send "Abandoned Hair Extensions 1st Email"

ON

Total revenue	AOV	Revenue/Person
$15454.84	$230.66	$7.08

Open rate	CTR	Unsubscribes
59.81%	12.74%	0.18%
(1305)	(278)	(4)

Updated 7 minutes ago

Needless to say, the most important component of a cart abandonment email is the ability to explain and give the customer clarity around your product and overcome common objections. You do this by reminding them about the quality of your products, your transparent return policy, guarantee, and if you can afford to also offer a discount, feel free to do that as well.

It may seem like a lot of different scenarios to cover, but you want to make sure that you convert all the customers that you can, and since these customers have already put something in their basket, they are already thinking of purchasing that item, so this email may just be that little push they need to buy from you.

Showcase Your Best Selling Items

Your best-selling items are the ones that are bought most frequently, and so they are the ones that you stock the most. These items will be the ones that repeat customers come back for and new customers are looking for. It is important to showcase these items so that customers can find them easily. You also want customers who are looking for something else to see your best-selling items because there is a high likelihood that they would be interested in these items too.

The first way to showcase your best-selling items is to have them on the homepage of your website, that way everyone that visits your website can easily see them. Label these products as your 'best-sellers' or 'most popular'.

The second way to showcase your best-selling items is to put them at the top, or even have them as the main feature of your marketing emails which I discussed earlier. Send an email that showcases these products, with their prices, and discusses all the features. If you can, add some reviews about the best sellers from previous customers and be sure to include a direct link to these items on the email so that the customer can immediately click and buy the product.

The third way to showcase these best-selling items is to showcase them on social media (if you are doing any social media advertising). Again, have pictures of the products with their prices, put a description of the items that say how great the quality of the product is, and add in some reviews from people who have bought the product. Include a direct link to the product on your website so that the customer can easily click on it and buy the product. This is a great way to bring in new customers, especially if you have used SEO (Search Engine Optimization) and these advertisements will appear on the screens of customers who have looked for similar products.

Last but not least, you can have specials or 1-2 day deals where you put your best-selling items on sale and let your customers know via social media and email. This not only encourages the customers to buy the product because it is a best-seller, but also because they can get it for slightly cheaper. This will also encourage repeat sales from previous customers who already love the product.

Your best-selling items can be used as an effective marketing tool because everybody wants what is popular, and if they are the best-selling items then they are definitely already popular with your existing client base, so you have a good chance of getting sales from them. Put them at the front of your website and your marketing and watch them sell even faster. Just be sure to check on your inventory to make sure you have enough quantities.

Showcase Reviews

Reviews are an important part of the selling process.

How many times have you bought (or not bought) something because of the great or terrible reviews that other customers have left on the product?

Ask customers who have bought your products to review the items they have bought. Send them an email asking them to review the items – if they love the items they will gladly write something positive about them. I usually give customers about 2-3 weeks before asking for a review, that way they have enough time to experience the product. Perhaps as an incentive to get customers to review their products, offer them a reward such as a chance to win a voucher for your store for each review that they leave.

Make sure that reviews by other customers can be seen on your website along with the product. You can also share your best reviews on social media and also when you send out emails to customers. We all look at product reviews when buying items and it should be the same for your products! So try to convince previous clients to leave reviews and make those reviews visible so that they can help convert new customers to buy the products too.

CHAPTER 5: MAKING YOUR BRAND STAND OUT

> *"Every great dream begins with a dreamer."* —
> *Harriet Tubman*

Build A Website!

There are so many hair extension websites out there these days that you need to put the time and effort in to make yours stand out above the rest. Here are some ideas that I have learned over the years on how to make sure that customers see your website first and that they remember it even after they have looked at countless other websites that offer similar products that you do. Don't make the mistake of thinking that your brand will 'sell itself'. You need to put in work and effort to make your brand stand out against other brands.

1. Have a website that looks great

It has been proven that in the first 3 seconds of viewing a website, a customer decides whether they are going to stay on it or leave it. This shows how important it is to have a website that looks beautiful and is user friendly and easy to navigate. You also want the look of your website to match your brand. A hair business should not look like an accounting website, but a place where you will find beautiful hair products. Choose colors, fonts, and themes that match your business's brand, and that leaves an impression on customers who visit the site. They should remember how beautiful your website is after they leave it.

2. Make sure your website is easy to use

Just as important as having a website that looks beautiful, you need to make sure that your website is user-friendly. If a potential customer finds it difficult to find what they are looking for then they are going to leave your site and go buy from someone else. Make sure that it is easy to search for items; that it is easy to view items with their images, descriptions, details, and reviews, and that the checkout process is easy to use. If a potential customer finds any of these to be difficult, they will become frustrated easily and leave.

3. Make sure to keep your website updated

Another thing that frustrates customers is slow websites that take a long time to load pages and images. Make sure that your website is built well and that its pages load quickly and that the images appear very quickly once the page is opened. Having to wait for these things will make potential customers impatient and they will leave your site. Make sure that your website is updated regularly and that it runs smoothly. You want to have the latest software available.

When you do maintenance on your website, try to do it at times when your customers are least likely to visit, because you will want to make sure your website is not in maintenance mode while you are working on it if they are coming to your site. You do not want to cause an inconvenience to potential buyers.

4. Have an online chat

Sometimes customers may have a question about a product or will simply like to know more about your products and your company, but they don't want to waste time doing research or waiting for a reply to an email. This is why it is important to have an online chat where customers can quickly and easily contact you. You don't want to lose a sale because a customer found faster information somewhere else. Having an online chat often closes deals for you, so it is important to have this feature on your website. This online chat is usually shown by an icon on the bottom right-hand side of all of the web pages on your website. Once a visitor clicks on this icon, a chat will open and customers will be able to message one of your customer service employees (or yourself when you are just getting started). Try to have someone on your online chat for as many hours of the day as possible, and make sure that when no one is there to reply, the online chat says that it is offline, and offers the customer the option to send an email that you can reply to later instead.

5. Have an FAQ section

Sometimes customers will have questions about

something and often many people will have the same questions (think of things like delivery times, refund policies, and order tracking). This is why having an FAQ section on your website will be helpful. Customers will be able to find the answers to their questions without having to contact you. Try to think of all the possible questions a customer could ask and put them in an FAQ, and if a customer comes to you with a new question, be sure to put that into the FAQ too as it is likely that someone else will have the same question. Having this section will save you and your customer time because the information is readily available to the customer so they don't have to go searching for it or use the online chat to ask about it. The FAQ section should give all of the answers to possible questions that a visitor might have and convert that visitor into a customer.

6. Be open to suggestions

Once a customer has checked out, have a review page where you ask the customer what their experience using the website was like. Ask them to rate how easy it was to find what they wanted, how they felt the page loading times were, how appealing they found the website, if they got stuck on anything, and for their overall opinion of the website, then offer them a chance to write any suggestions that they may have. View these reviews and use common suggestions to improve your website when you make new updates for it. Remember that you do not have to change your website according to every comment made, but if there is a common theme (such as the images taking too long to load) then be sure to fix that. Customers like to feel heard and they will be delighted to see that you have used their suggestions, which will likely turn customers into repeat customers.

If you are feeling worried about not knowing how to create your own website and have a domain name, then do not worry! I will show you exactly how to do this in later chapters, so don't give up now, keep on reading!

Your Business's Name

Your business name is so important. It is the first thing about your brand that people remember. Having a business name that is easy to remember is important to have repeat customers and to bring in new customers. Having a brand that is difficult to remember will make it hard for customers to remember who you are and to come back to you.

Your name needs to be something simple, original, catchy, and memorable. A fifth-grader should be able to remember and spell your business name. You want customers to search for your business name on any internet search engine and be able to find you easily.

If a potential customer hears your name when a friend recommends your business to them, you want them to remember it later when they can search for you. If a potential customer sees advertising by you (on social media, magazine pages, or anywhere else that you advertise), you also want them to remember your name and to search for you later. If a customer who is wearing your hair gets a compliment on it, you want them to say, "Thanks! I got it from Wealthy

Hair!" and not, "Thanks, I got it off a website, but I can't remember their name."

It is also important to have a domain name that relates well to your business name. It would be difficult to find the company 'Wealthy Hair' online if its domain name was something like 'lacefront-wig.com' as they do not relate. Try to have your business name in your domain name or ideally both to be the same so that when customers search for you from their search engines they will be able to find you easily.

So be careful when coming up with your business and your domain name. A great way to make it memorable is to have an accompanying logo with the name in it. This will help customers remember your name and be able to recognize it.

Clear Product Pictures

Pictures are so important when selling products online, if you do not have pictures of your products, you will not sell much! We all want to know exactly what something looks like before we buy it – simply having a description is not enough.

Your pictures need to be high quality and display well on your website. You don't need a professional photographer, but you do need to make sure that the pictures of your items are in good lighting. When it comes to hair extensions, you want to make sure that the hair is clearly visible and the type, style, and length of the hair can clearly be seen. You need a picture of each and every item that you sell!

If you are selling bundle packs, you need to take pictures of the items that you are selling in the bundle together so that customers can see each piece that the bundle contains.

You need to have a picture next to every item that you sell – the more pictures of the item, the better. You can have pictures of hair extensions lying on their own, or on a model head, or on a person's head. The last two offer you lots of opportunities to take pictures of the hair at different angles and to show it off while it is styled.

Make sure that your pictures are taken with a high-quality camera, there is no point in having a beautiful website when your pictures are low resolution!

Pictures are what really sell eCommerce products so they are very important. Remember to put them on the homepage of your website and on any email or social media marketing to immediately draw the attention of your customers. The more pictures that you have of each product the better because this allows the customer to see exactly what they are buying, instead of having doubts about whether or not the product is what they want. Pictures might be what closes many deals for you.

Suggest Complementary Products

This is yet another super tip that I have learned to do over the years that has increased my profits by so much! When a customer looks at a product or puts it into their basket, it is a good idea to have suggestions for complementary products. For example, you could suggest shampoos and conditioners when a customer looks at hairpieces. This is an easy way to make more money per customer.

Suggesting products can help customers see products that they had not thought of buying, and encourage them to look at and buy them. Customers may be delighted to find that you have products that they did not think you had.

Before a customer proceeds to payment, you can also have a page that suggests other products to put into their basket. These items can be random selections from the website or they can be targeted based on what the customer has in their basket.

Suggesting complementary products can easily increase your profits by 30% to 40% by drawing the customer's attention to the fact that there are other items that they may not have seen or thought to look for. So make sure that you have suggestions linked to every product on your website.

Email List Building

This is something that I wish someone had told me to do earlier. I only started to build my email list long after I started my business and I can only imagine how many sales I have lost out on because I did not start doing this sooner!

To build an email list, you can either have a pop-up on your website's homepage that invites visitors to opt-in to receiving marketing emails from you, or you can have a checkbox at checkout where customers can choose to opt-in to receive these emails.

Building an email list is a great tool to keep you connected to your customers. It helps you tell them when you are having sales or discounts and it can serve as a reminder about your website and your products.

Email lists can be used to contact customers to ask them to write reviews for your products which, as I discussed before, is very important.

Emails can also be used to offer promotional coupons such as birthday coupons or any other special deals that you have.

Receiving a promotional email often reminds customers that they would like to buy from your store again and prompts them to do so. Therefore, it is so important to include links on your emails that take the customer straight to your website, and even to the specific products that you are promoting,

Email lists also allow you to communicate with your customers by writing blogs or educational pieces about your products. These will help teach your customers about your products which may encourage them to buy new products.

Having an email list is a great tool as it is a free way to advertise your website, communicate with your customers, and offer promotions and discounts that customers will love. It will also encourage customers who have looked at your website but not bought anything to take another look and buy.

Mobile-Friendly Websites And Applications

There are so many people who will prefer to use the convenience of their phones to buy from your website. This is why it is so important to have a mobile-friendly website. This is something that you will have to ask your web designers to do for you – they need to make a website that is fully functional, looks great, and is easy to use on a mobile phone.

It has been shown that the majority of online buyers use their mobile phones to make online shopping orders, and this is why you want a website that customers will find easy to use on their mobile phones.

Another option is to have a mobile application for your business made. This will cost you more as you will need a mobile app developer to make the app for you but it may be worth it. Having an app that allows you to easily find what you want, purchase it, and then track the order is a major convenience of eCommerce that will help you close sales even while you are sleeping.

Have a rewards system such as coupons or cashback when customers spend a certain amount of money. Customers will be able to easily see how far they are from receiving their reward and they can easily access their reward code from your site.

Mobile is the future and you should definitely make your business mobile. Having a mobile-friendly website and application makes it so easy for customers to buy from you anytime and anywhere. This is especially useful if a customer recommends your products to someone else! They can quickly and easily show that person your website or application and that person might just be your next customer because they can buy from you immediately.

Selling Through Education

If you look at my website, WealthyHair.com, you will see that I have many blogs and tips that are free and easy to access for my customers. Customers love reading and seeing this information because it shows that your business knows what they are doing and they provide helpful hints and tips on what to buy and how to use your products – increasing your sales!

Writing blog posts, posting on social media, creating emails, creating vlogs, and writing articles are just some of the ways that you can write about your products to educate customers and inspire them to buy your product. Doing all of these costs nothing but your time and effort, and customers will appreciate it and will likely become more loyal to you for it.

Customers will love that you are giving them tips and tricks on how to use your products to their best potential and they will be more willing to stay with a brand that communicates with them and provides them with information and helpful tips.

You can create content that helps customers decide which product is the best for them, how to best use the product, provide them with some industry secrets, give reviews of your products, offer specials that can be redeemed by viewing the content you provide, and even offer a Q&A section where customers can submit questions that you answer in the next edition of your content.

You can create this content on a daily, weekly, bimonthly, or monthly basis, the more the better. Customers like to know that they can read your new articles every Friday or watch a new video on how to use your products every Wednesday, or even both! You are not limited to doing only one type of content and the topics that you can cover are endless.

This content will make customers more loyal to you as they will have learned about a certain product from you, and will therefore think that you deserve the sale. Providing this content for free is a nice way to stay in touch with your customers and help you get more sales.

Offer The Highest-Quality Hair Extensions

I have learned the hard way that this is an area that you simply cannot compromise on. Having the best quality products is the way to get your brand to stand out among the rest. The best way to keep customers is to provide them with the best possible quality products that are out there. Customers do not want to pay for hair that will start shedding after one wash – they want something that they can rely on to look beautiful for a few months.

The best way to out-sell your competitors is to sell the

best quality. Do quality checks on every batch of hair that you buy from a vendor to ensure that you are consistently sending out great-quality products. This will build trust with your clients who will return to you every few months for their hair extensions.

If you offer other products on your website, make sure that these products are top quality too. There is no point in selling high-quality hair extensions but the shampoo that your customer buys with it is terrible – your customer will remember that the shampoo was terrible and not that the extensions were great and you may lose a repeat customer. Make sure that everything you sell is of the quality that you want related to your brand.

High-quality is what you want your brand to be all about. You want a reputation of selling only the best products out there, so do not try to shortcut or compromise on this!

Tell Your Story

It is always nice to know where the business you are buying from came from and how it has been built and developed over the years to become the great business that it is today.

I am very open about who I am, where I come from, and how I got my business started. This is because I want people to know exactly who they are buying from. Writing a short 'about us' or 'about me' article on your website helps customers get to know you and to appreciate where you came from and what your goals for your business are.

Customers will love knowing the true story behind a company and how it has come to be the way that it is. This is also the perfect place to thank your customers for their support. This article will inspire customers to buy from you as they will feel like they know you on a more personal level, and that they would like to support your goals and where you would like to take the company.

For example, I love to tell people about how I had to sell my own furniture to get my business started – it shows how dedicated and committed I was to starting this company, and how strongly I want it to succeed. I like my customers to know that I have been through all of the trial and error of owning this business and that is why it is a success today. I also make sure to tell my customers that my goal for my business has always been to sell high-quality hair. It shows that I care about the quality of my products and that I will do everything I can to provide my customers with only the best products.

So, whatever your story is, share it with your customers. It will make them feel like they know you and that they want to help you achieve your business goals.

Alert: Just a friendly reminder to register for my FREE masterclass where I will be sharing strategies on how to start your own branded hair business without feeling overwhelmed and with minimum investment.

Go here to save your spot:
WealthyHair.com/Webinar

Chapter 6: Elevating Your Customer Experience

"I'm hungry for knowledge. The whole thing is to learn every day, to get brighter and brighter. That's what this world is about. You look at someone like Gandhi, and he glowed. Martin Luther King glowed. Muhammad Ali glows. I think that's from being bright all the time, and trying to be brighter."
— Jay-Z

Leverage Social Media

Social media is an incredible tool that can be used to a huge advantage in the eCommerce world. Social media allows you to easily interact with customers, have free advertising, post blogs/vlogs/articles/tips that remind the customer about your brand and entice the customer to buy your products over your competitors.

Having social media accounts is absolutely necessary in this day and age for any business because not only can you communicate with your potential customers, you can also get feedback from them.

Facebook, Twitter, and Instagram are the top three social media platforms that your business should be on. All of your accounts should be professional and complement your brand. If you are running a hair business, you want to create a professional page for your company. Your profile descriptions should explain exactly what your business is – who you are, what you sell, and what goals your business has (for example, to sell the best-quality hair extensions in the area).

As you are most likely aware, you can also start a YouTube account where you can upload things like tutorial videos or reviews from happy customers. This also provides a great platform where customers can ask questions about your business and your products – just make sure that you answer these questions.

Customers like to reach out to businesses when they have a question and this is why it is important to be active on your social media, they will expect fast replies from someone who is knowledgeable in the company and its products. If your posts receive any comments, the person managing the accounts should reply to the comments, even if it is a simple, "Thank you" in response to a positive comment. The customer will feel personally heard if you reply to their comment, and this will make the customer want to buy from you because you are making an effort to connect with them – this is customer service in the eCommerce world!

And our goal is to always have great customer service, right? This means that it is especially important to reply when someone posts something negative or just posts a suggestion. Replying will make the customer feel better about their complaint and may shop with you again because they are happy you addressed the issue and that you care about their experience with your company.

Being active on social media also involves posting content. If you are having a promotion, post about it, if you are selling new products, post about it. You can post daily tips and tricks, or daily articles about your products, you can show off product reviews, or provide links to articles and blogs that are on your website. Being active on social media keeps you top of mind with potential customers and people are always more loyal to companies they see and are able to interact with on a daily basis.

With marketing, you can invest in two ways, you can take the time to do it or invest the money to hire someone to do it for you. If posting on social media seems like a lot of work, I suggest you hire somebody such as a social media manager who knows social media and how all of the platforms work. This person can post daily and reply to questions or comments quickly as their focus will be on managing the social media accounts.

Make sure that the person who is in charge of your social media accounts responds in a customer-service-friendly manner. They should be polite to customers and respond to any messages or comments with a friendly tone. You don't want nasty responses to comments being sent around on social media!

We are living in a world of social media and technology. Having an expert to make your brand visible to the world of social media is almost vital to surviving as a brand these days. The first thing that a person does when they find a company is to search for it on social media, so make sure that you can be easily found and that what they find is positive, promotes your brand, and convinces people to buy from you.

Online Chat

Have you ever been doing some online shopping and wanted to know something about a product that's not in the description? Maybe an item is out of stock and you want to know when they are restocking their items. However, there was no available help to answer your questions? You probably went to another website to shop there, right?

This is where having an online chat comes in handy – it is the equivalent of having an in-store employee who can answer any questions. Online chat appears as a message board at (usually) the bottom right side of the website. This should be available on every page of the website and the customer should be able to click on it at any time and type a message. This message will appear on your or your customer service screen and you or your assistant can quickly type an answer that the customer will immediately see.

In most cases, the most common questions asked on chat are pertaining to product attributes, delivery and pricing. We end up selling to over 30% of the people that use our website online chat software. So as you can see, chatting with customers while they are on your website is very important.

If you do hire someone to monitor the chat for you, please make sure that whoever is monitoring your online chat has access to all of the details of your business, and can also quickly contact you regarding questions that they do not have the answer to. In order to give fast replies to questions, the person who is answering needs to know or have fast access to the answer. If the person managing the online chat does not know anything about the business, then there is no point in having it. You also need to make sure that anyone who communicates via the online chat is courteous, friendly, and responds politely to the customer. Nobody wants bad customer service – even if they are buying online.

An online chat is an essential tool that makes the online shopping world even more accessible and desirable to the customer. This is part of your customer service so be sure your customers have an outstanding experience while using it.

Tutorials

Short videos are a great way to communicate with customers because they will grab their visual and their hearing senses, think of the adverts that you see on TV – they grab your attention, help you learn about a product, and convince you to buy the product. Tutorials are a similar concept, but last for a few minutes rather than a few seconds.

Tutorials are videos that are between 3 and 30 minutes long that explain something to you. These are a new trend and a way to capture new and existing audiences to your product.

Tutorials are a great way to keep your customers engaged and to encourage them to buy from you. You can make tutorials about anything related to your products or your business. A great idea is to make tutorials that show customers how to use the products – installation, coloring, styling, and maintenance. Something else that your tutorials can focus on is doing comparisons of your products to help customers choose the best product for them – this will convert many customers because it will motivate them to buy products that they know are right for them.

Your tutorials can be posted on your website or on other platforms such as YouTube, TikTok, and Instagram Reels. When you upload a new tutorial, send an email to your email list describing what the tutorial contains and add a link that takes the customer straight to the webpage where your tutorial is. You can also post snippets of your tutorials on social media, post a piece of the video that will show what the tutorial is about, and encourage your followers to click on a link to watch the full video.

Customers appreciate tutorials from the business that sells their products and also increases trust in the company.

You also need to remember to look at any comments

posted on your tutorial videos – customers will tell you what they loved and what they didn't love about the video and whether or not it helped them. They may also ask extra questions about the video that you should respond to. Use these comments to make your future tutorials even better!

Tutorials are quickly becoming a big and important way to close sales these days. They can be the difference between you and another company, and they definitely elevate your customers' experience with your company.

Get Feedback

Good customer service is what will get customers to return to you. If a customer has a good experience buying from you, then they will be happy to buy from you again and they will be happy to recommend you to their friends.

So to provide the best possible customer experience, you need to ask customers what they want. How will you know whether customers enjoy their experience on your website if you don't ask?

A few days after a customer purchases something from you, the best way to get their feedback is to send them an email. In this email, have a quick survey that simply asks customers to rate their experience and offer them the opportunity to make suggestions. It is important to make this survey short – customers don't want to spend 10 minutes filling out a survey. You want your survey to take less than 2 minutes to fill out – this greatly increases the chances of getting customers to fill out the survey and complete it.

Another way that you can get feedback is to have a survey after a customer finishes their payment. Again, this has to be a quick survey that the customer can fill out in a couple of minutes. This is probably where you will get the most reviews from customers as they will see it as part of the checkout process and will be willing to quickly fill out a survey. However, this does not give the customer an opportunity to provide you with feedback on your items (because they don't have the product yet). This survey will be focused on their experience of using your website and their shopping experience, which is still extremely important!

It can sometimes be hard to get customers to fill out surveys. For them, it is an inconvenience and takes up their time – even though for you it is a really helpful tool. Putting the survey at the end of a purchase will convince more customers to do it, but that still does not guarantee that the majority of your customers will fill out your surveys. A great idea to get your customers to fill out your surveys via email is to offer them a reward – a free gift during their next purchase, an entry into a prize draw, or a small coupon will convince more customers to fill out the survey.

Did you know that most happy customers do not fill out surveys? In case you find that most of your surveys are negative, it is only because those who are happy with the website felt no need to fill out the survey. Take the suggestions and comments that you receive to improve your website, but remember that you also have happy customers.

At the end of the day, customers want to feel heard and know that you value their business, so asking them for a survey will increase the chances of customers returning to your site and recommending you to other people.

Make sure to thank any customer who has filled out a survey with a quick 'Thank you!' page that pops up after they have submitted the survey. Remember, these people are taking time to help you better your service and your products.

Focus On Personalization

Making your website stand out is an important way to leave a good impression on potential customers and to out-sell your competition. Before building your website, and even before you start building your brand, do your homework. Find the best performing brands and take on their ideas to build your brand. Part of this is making shopping online a personal and enjoyable service for each and every customer. Get to know your customers on a personal level, learn their names and find out what is important to them. Be genuine with your customers instead of making them feel like you are always trying to sell to them. Think of this as if you are providing your customers with a personal shopper experience.

Pay attention to what your customers buy, what they are buying it for, and why they choose certain products over others. This will allow you to offer them personalized offers (especially for special occasions, such as their birthday). This will also help you to make recommendations to the customer, show them new products that you have stocked that they will be interested in, and ultimately help them find the best products for them.

Customers love to feel like they are being cared for and remembered. Simply remembering small details about a customer will make them feel like they have made a friend who they would like to support. Having a relationship like this with your customers will make them more open and honest about the things about your business that they like, and more importantly, where they think you could improve.

I would like to give you a quick example of what I usually do in my business. Lucille, one of my long term customers, had told me that she was having surgery. On the day of her surgery, I surprised her by sending her flowers to the hospital. The great rapport that I have with Lucille is because I took the time and effort to get to know her, and through this she let me know that she was having surgery. I wanted to let her know that she was appreciated and that we care about her. This is the high level of personalization will for sure bring customers back to you every time.

Another example that I can give you is my customer, Cheryl. She knew that I was born in Kenya because we had talked about our lives with each other, and Cheryl often told me how much she wanted to visit Kenya. So, on my next visit to Kenya, I bought her some African-themed earrings and bracelets that she loved. This helped to strengthen the bond between Cheryl and I and therefore the bond between Cheryl and Wealthy Hair. Gestures like this are what makes a customer loyal and want to support you. Customers appreciate when you do things like this for them, and who knows, maybe the customer will do something personally nice for you too. Cheryl will also tell her friends and people she knows about where her jewelry came from when she wears it – and she will tell those people about the great customer service of Wealthy Hair.

Everybody loves to be treated as if they are special and important to a business that they buy from. This is why you should treat every customer as if they are a friend, rather than just a customer. This will not only improve your customer experience but it will also make running your own business more enjoyable because you will get to know many wonderful people.

CHAPTER 7: MISTAKES TO AVOID

"Learn from the mistakes of others. You can't live long enough to make them all yourself."
— *Eleanor Roosevelt*

Competing On Price Only

Yes, I totally get it, we all start a business so that we can make a profit and also a difference. While profit is the goal, having the most customers buying from you because you have slightly lower prices than your competitors is not the way to achieve that goal. Someone will always be willing to sell at a lower price than you, to the point where your profits will drop significantly. You should still do your homework before starting your business to determine what kind of pricing your competitors offer, but do not let this become the determining factor in your pricing. Having the lowest prices may get you some customers that choose you instead of your competitors, but your focus on ways to get more customers should be based on other factors instead of pricing. This is what gets you repeat customers rather than one-off customers, and also gets you more customers because of recommendations and reviews!

The first thing that you should focus on to get more customers than your competitors is quality. Your competitors may be selling products that are worth a lot less than yours, and are therefore able to sell them for cheaper. Is this the kind of business that you want to have? Of course not! You want a business that offers the best *quality* products because once customers have tried out your products, they will never want to go back to the cheap quality of your competitors. This is what will get you repeat customers. So, make sure that you do quality assurance tests on every product that you sell. You want every customer loving their hair extensions, so they keep coming back to you over and over again.

Customer experience is the other thing that you should focus on to get customers and to get customers coming back to your business. Anyone can walk into a beauty supply store and get hair extensions (usually low quality), but they are not likely to receive great customer service or any service at all! Being treated rudely, being followed around, and being treated like you are an inconvenience are the main reasons you have a great opportunity to succeed in the hair extension industry. You must still deliver awesome customer service even on your eCommerce website.

Having features such as an online chat, or even just an email or phone number where customers can contact your business counts as customer service because of the way that you speak to customers during these interactions and how quickly you reply to customers affects their experience. So be sure to have ways for customers to contact your business, and make sure that your responses are polite and courteous, and that these responses are provided as quickly as possible. When it comes to delivery, make sure that you ship the packages to your customers as soon as possible to allow fast delivery.

These are more important things to your business than having the lowest price. Your business will automatically thrive when you have great quality products and excellent customer service. You will be surprised to find out how many customers are willing to pay extra for excellent quality and a welcoming experience. This is how you can build recurring income in your business by having repeat customers. If you are like me and you do not want to hustle for every dollar you get, this is the way to go.

Selling Cheap Quality

I have said it before and now I am saying it again – the quality of the products that you are selling is so important! You simply cannot sell low-quality items and expect to succeed in the massive industry of selling hair extensions. This is something that I wish somebody had told me when I started my business. When I tried to sell average-quality hair in the beginning, my business almost failed and I realized that this was because there were so many other places that were selling hair that was the same quality as mine. This is why I spent 3 months traveling the world to find the best-quality hair that is available *in the world* to sell to my customers!

Quality is what will make you survive in this industry – it is an $8 billion industry and only those who offer the best to their customers will stand the test of time. Selling cheap quality items will not bring customers back to you, especially if they find better quality from one of your competitors! It may be tempting to sell cheap quality products – you can sell it for cheaper to customers, you can purchase the inventory for cheaper, and you won't have to invest as much money to get your business started. This is all great – if you want your business to fail within a few months if not weeks!

You need to think about the future, about having regular customers in a year's time, about having your customers be proud of their hair, about your customers telling their friends where they got their hair extensions from. None of these will happen if you are selling cheap, low-quality hair extensions that shed and lose their great look after one wash. You want your customers to glow in their hair extensions, not struggle to brush it without it shedding!

Although it may seem like a big investment to start your business, it will be worth it to start out with great-quality hair. It may be harder to get some customers at first, but eventually, they will all come to you looking for the great hair that their friend was wearing at a party the previous week. In the long run, you will see that the strategy of selling cheap-quality hair that anyone can get for a few dollars at a beauty supply store will not yield a successful business in the long run but selling hair that is great quality and looks beautiful will become a very successful, life-changing business.

Cheaper is not always better and that is exactly the case when it comes to selling hair extensions. Quality is king in the hair extension industry because it is such a huge industry. So many stores and online stores are selling hair extensions that are 'acceptable' or just okay quality. You need to stand out from the rest, and the best way to do that is to have products that offer much better quality than your competitors. People are so willing to pay extra for something if they know that they are getting the best quality that is out there!

I cannot stress enough how important it is to have the best quality products on the market. You want to be proud of the products that you are selling and you want your customers to be happy with every purchase!

Selling To Fraudulent Customers

This is another mistake that I have had to learn to deal with the hard way. Unfortunately, fraudulent customers are everywhere, and having an eCommerce business makes you more vulnerable to these fraudulent customers.

The best way to deal with these customers is to stop them before they can even attempt to do anything on your website. Ask your web developer to make sure that firewalls, and other safety measures are in place to prevent any 'bots' from getting access to your website.

The next thing to do to prevent any fraud on your website is to only use trusted methods of payment. Some trusted methods include PayPal, Visa, Mastercard, Discover, and American Express. These services are trusted and can be used all over the world and they will make sure that you get your money safely, and that no one can access your banking details.

Using trusted payment methods also makes the customer feel more at ease when they make a payment to you.

You also want to be careful with customers who ask for favors such as, "If you send it to me now, I will pay some of the price now and the rest of it later." I would recommend that you do not do this, because every time I have EVER done it, I have lost money and as a result, I do not offer that option at all. You can always recommend pay later services such as PayPal and/or customers can use their credit card. Initially, It may feel like you are losing out on a sale and not offering good customer service to turn a customer down, but it is a huge risk to not get the full payment of a sale, so rather be safe than sorry.

Make sure that you use protective measures on your website to ensure that fraudulent customers cannot access your details from your website, watch out for any suspicious activity from customers, and make sure that you have secure, well-known, and trusted methods of payment.

Not Following Up With Past Customers

It is well-known in the business world that getting a customer to return to you is easier and cheaper than getting a new customer. In this regard then, it is super important to follow up with your customers who have purchased from your website.

When customers are in the checkout process on your website, you should ask customers to provide their email so that you can send them a receipt of their order and other updates to enhance their experience with your company.

Another way to keep customers returning is to have a loyalty program where you offer a small in store credit for a certain amount of money that the customer purchases. This will encourage customers to return to you because they know that they will be getting a reward when they shop frequently with you. You can send your customers monthly emails reminding them of their cashback allowance so that they remember you when they need to buy something that you offer on your website.

You want all of your customers to buy from you every time they need products that you sell so making sure that the customer is encouraged to return to your website is so important. Offer customers rewards to encourage them to buy from you again and again and make sure to follow up with your customers to make sure that they remember you and feel heard and valued by you.

Not Creating An Email List

As I said before, creating an email list is probably one of the most powerful marketing tools that you can have, and it is very affordable to do so! This is something that I wish that I had started so much earlier in my business because I could have collected so many more emails and made so many more sales if I had started my email list at the very beginning when I started my business.

You can ask any customer who visits your website to enter their email to be a part of your email list – make sure to ask your web designer to have a banner or a pop up that asks the visitor for their email information on your website's homepage. To encourage visitors to enter their email, offer them a coupon or a small discount on their first purchase if they sign up.

I would encourage you to keep in contact with your email list at least twice a month so you can always stay at the top of their mind. The initial discount that you give customers on their first purchase for giving you their email will encourage them to make that first purchase and close the deal on a sale!

The marketing emails that you send to everyone on your email list need to be designed in a way that converts customers – it needs to look beautiful and relatable to your brand, be informative about your products, and offer direct links to items on your website. Think of how many times you have opened an email with an item being advertised that you loved so much that you immediately clicked on the link and bought the item. That's exactly what you want your customers to do!

Since the goal of your email list is to get customers to make a purchase, you are going to make a lot of sales that you wouldn't have made if you did not send the customer the email. These emails can add to your monthly profit by 30% to 40%, which is huge!

Your email list also lets customers know when you are having specials and discounts which often convinces customers to make a purchase, especially if you are having a special discount for specific events such as New Year's Eve, or even the customer's birthday! So imagine how many people you can convince to buy from you just by the click of an email.

You can also use your email lists to let customers know that you have released a new blog article/video/tutorial/ magazine, or anything else that you make to connect with your customers. Remember to include direct links to what you have released so that they can easily access it.

Email marketing will help you increase your sales and I really want you to start building your email list as soon as you start your business because it is one of the most important assets your brand can have.

Giving Up Too Quickly

Guys, it took me months and months of hard work, of trying different things and failing, exploring the world, and even selling my furniture to make my business successful! After 18 months of facing many failures and challenges, I almost gave up on my business, but I am so glad that I didn't! My goal of this book is to let you know the best secrets of the hair extension industry so that you do not make the same mistakes that I did, but this is still not a set it and forget it type of thing!

Even with all of the advice that I have given you, you might still make mistakes and learn things the hard way, and go through hard times before your business becomes successful – but this does not mean that you should give up!

The success of your business could be right around the corner, and if you give up too soon then you are giving up an incredible chance to change your life.

You will need to work hard and spend a lot of time and money on your business to become successful. Sometimes this may be hard and will make you want to give it all up, but I am begging you not to! I truly believe that you can do this!

No one has ever built a successful business in a day, in fact, it usually takes at least multiple months of consistency to become successful. I hope that with all the information that I have shared with you in this book, I have shortened your success curve. My hope is that you use my years of experience in this industry and my mistakes to get that extra edge! I have made all of the mistakes for you, but you will still have to put the work in and remember to not give up.

If you are feeling nervous about starting your business, then keep reading this book because later on, I will provide you with everything I can to help you get started the right way the first time!

Chapter 8: Mindset Hacks For Successful Hair Entrepreneurs

❧

> *"Five days a week, I read my goals before I go to sleep and when I wake up. There are 10 goals around health, family, and business with expiration dates, and I update them every six months."*
> — *Daymond John*

How To Keep Going

Starting your own business is challenging for everyone. In fact, I have yet to come across any successful entrepreneur who has not had their fair share of challenges. One of my main reasons for writing this book is because of all my struggles that I had and me wanting to help other aspiring hair entrepreneurs shorten their success curve. I highly recommend that you make a decision to be committed to do whatever it takes to make your dream of having a successful hair business a reality.

Remember, the only way to fail is to stop trying. That's why I am going to show you important mindset habits that you should have before you start building your business. You need to be in the best mindset that gives you the motivation and inspiration every day to get up and work towards your goal of running a successful business.

Acknowledging and Reprogramming Your Mindset

Having the right mindset is crucial to achieving success in your business. Let's look at how you can achieve this.

Step 1: Mindset - The A.C.C. Method

I would like to introduce you to the Wealthy Hair methodology that has helped thousands of hair entrepreneurs achieve the right mindset. I call it the **A.C.C. Method: Acknowledge, Challenge, and Change.**

1. **Acknowledge your beliefs:** Ask yourself what limiting beliefs you have – now or in the past. For example, I was always told that money doesn't grow on trees growing up and as a result, I had a scarcity mentality concerning money.

2. **Challenge your beliefs:** Make yourself a belief statement – this statement should make you believe that you deserve to make more money, have more freedom, and that you can change and impact the world in a positive way. Ask yourself why not you? And why not now? For example, I believe that I deserve and can make a difference in my customers' lives.

3. **Change your beliefs:** Imagine all of the things that you can do once you have more money. Maybe you can finally take that vacation you have always wanted to! Maybe you can stay home more and be there for your loved ones! You can also give back to the charities you care about.

Complete this sentence now:

With more money I will…

Step 2: Set Your Goal

Having a goal makes you accountable, helps you not overthink, over analyze and procrastinate.

Decide what your goal is and when you will complete it. For example, fill in the blanks for the sentence:

I will complete (goal) _____ by (due date) _____.

Step 3: Make Your Goals Real

Write down your goal statement somewhere that you will see daily. Believe that you too can have a thriving hair business.

Fail-Proof Hacks To Stay Motivated

Sometimes it is really hard to stay motivated. You may get tired and feel discouraged that your efforts are not bringing in the desired results. Please know that it is okay to feel this way, even the most successful entrepreneurs feel like this sometimes. I know that I have struggled on some days to find the motivation to do what needs to be done for my business.

This is why you need to train your brain to keep going and remember that motivation is the driving force behind success, this is why having hacks to stay motivated is so important. Some things that will help keep you motivated include exercise, praying, meditation, thinking of the future, writing down your goal, and keep doing all the things that make you positive, motivated, and happy. Here are my five secrets to staying motivated:

1. **Avoid becoming overwhelmed by breaking down your goals**: Figure out what your main long-term goal is, then break that goal into smaller short-term goals that will eventually add up to your long-term goal.

2. **Start your day right:** Have a morning ritual that will make you excited for the day ahead – write down your goals for the day and list 3 things that you want to accomplish each day.

3. **Set deadlines:** Setting a deadline is an important part of setting your goals because putting a timeline on your goals adds pressure and prevents procrastination. You need to have an attitude of, "I will get it done, whatever it takes!"

4. **Pay attention and keep track of your feelings**: When you notice that you are feeling unmotivated or very motivated, take note of what activities you

have been doing, what you have had to eat and drink, what thoughts you have had, and who you have been around. If you notice any patterns between any of these and the times that you feel unmotivated or motivated, then do something to change it if it makes you unmotivated, and keep doing it if it makes you feel motivated.

5. **What is your why?** You must have a compelling reason why you want to have a successful hair business and you should remind yourself of the consequences of giving up on your dreams. Would you be happier if 1 year from now you were in the same exact place financially and mentally? Be clear on your reasons for pursuing entrepreneurship. Are you doing this to spend more time with your loved ones? Or to travel and see the world? Or do you want more time and freedom for yourself? Your 'whys' are the reasons you will keep going when it becomes challenging.

6. **My sixth secret to staying motivated starts at the foundation of everything – Self-Care.** Sometimes we lose focus of our self-care because we are so concentrated on achieving our goals, and this is not good! Self-care is a must! So here are some tips to improve your self-care:

- Acknowledge how far you have come and what you have achieved so far.
- Ask yourself what things have you done lately that

make you feel good.

- What did someone thank you for recently?
- Recognize that negative thoughts and regrets will only keep you from moving forward, so try to move past these thoughts.
- Forgive yourself and start again however many times you need to. Every new day is an opportunity to start again.

Some final tips on motivation from me are:

1. Whenever you do something, ask yourself, "How is this action moving me closer to the life that I want for me and/or my family?"
2. Always start with the end in mind and break down all your major goals into smaller steps.
3. Surround yourself with people who lift you up and support your goals, and avoid negative people and those who always tear you down.

Motivation is a key factor that takes you up the ladder to success. Without motivation to do something, you will lose the ability to get up and do it every day. After being on this entrepreneurship journey since 2007, I have shared these tips so that you can wake up every day feeling motivated and inspired to keep going after your dreams. Always know that you deserve the life of your dreams and success is your birthright.

Becoming A Better Entrepreneur Through Challenges And Failures

Every single entrepreneur in the world, regardless of how successful they are, has failed many times on their journey. Challenges and failures are a part of the journey of learning and becoming a better person, founder, creator, or whatever else you want to be.

I faced many challenges and I failed many times when I first started my business – I started my whole business from scratch, I fell for scams and lost money, I bought inventory that never sold and lost money, I had to learn how to find clientele without the help of a mentor, I had to sell my furniture to keep my business hopes alive, and the list goes on and on! After 18 months of this I almost quit but then I realized that I have worked so hard for my dreams that I could not give up now. I used all of those challenges and failures as opportunities to learn instead of quitting. I can confidently say that I failed all the way to the top. I have come to accept failure as part of growth and I look at my failures as lessons on what not to do. My failures have helped me be innovative and thereby helping me build a multi-million dollar hair company.

It is important to remember that the challenges along your journey will drive innovation within you and self-improvement by opening new doors and ways of thinking. Overthinking the possibilities of failures leads to inaction and getting stuck, or even giving up, on your journey.

Here is the truth – you are going to mess up at some point! Even if you think that you have organized and planned everything perfectly, there will be days where things go wrong! But you need to realize that this is just normal and unavoidable, and the best thing to do for this is to keep your head up high, learn any lessons that you can from this, and carry on.

Everybody's journey is different so I cannot give you advice on every possible challenge or failure that you might face, but I want you to know that you can and should face your challenges head-on and embrace your failures as learning opportunities!

"I have missed more than 9,000 shots in my career. I have lost almost 300 games. On 26 occasions I have been entrusted to take the game-winning shot, and I missed. I've failed over and over again in my life." - Michael Jordan.

This quote by an extremely successful basketball player, Michael Jordan, proves how inevitable failures are on your road to success. You will have challenges and failures throughout your career as a business owner, but that is just part of the game, and it does not mean that you are not successful – it means that you are a human who is doing their best to live life on their own terms by going after their dreams.

Chapter 9: Ways To Fund Your Hair Business

~~~~

> *"If you have a dream AND you have a job. That's amazing! You can learn how to navigate both. Your employer, or as I like to call it your 'investor', gives you the money to invest in your dream, and pay your bills while you chase your dreams."*
> — Lisa Nichols

If you are strapped for cash, it takes some creativity to come up with ways to get the money you need to invest and start your business. I can relate to this because I had to sell furniture to help fund my dream of starting a hair business.

It is difficult but possible to keep a full-time job and start your own business if you are willing to be patient and you can commit to working extra hours after your daily work. I recommend that you do not quit your day job until your business can support your daily life and bills.

I have listed below some creative ways to come up with the money that you need to help you get started with your hair business.

Selling Unwanted Things In Your Garage

This is a great way to build funds to start your business and declutter your garage! When you have time, go to the garage and go through everything that you have stored inside it. Make one pile of things that you use often and want to keep, and make another pile for things that you no longer need and can get rid of.

Then you can put all of the stuff that you no longer need outside with a price on it and let people come by with offers to buy your stuff, or you can take all of your unwanted items to a store that buys second-hand things and see what they offer you! There are so many places online that you can sell your unwanted items now like Facebook Marketplace, Craigslist, LetGo, eBay, and countless others.

It's crazy how much value people will find in things that you no longer use. Who knows, you might raise enough money to start your own hair business and even have enough left over to go out to a fine restaurant for dinner.

Uber Or Lyft

If you have your own car and love driving, then why not join a company such as Uber or Lyft to earn some extra money? These jobs allow you to have flexible work hours and the majority of what you earn is from tips, so if you put in the effort to make your customers happy, you will make more money!

Credit Card Or PayPal Pay Later

You also have other options where you can invest now and then make monthly payments. The most popular ones I have come across are PayPal Pay Later and using a credit card. This method allows you to get the ball rolling with your business immediately instead of working for months and years to earn enough money to start.

DoorDash

Another great way to raise money to get started is DoorDash. They operate an online food ordering and food delivery platform. The good thing is the hours are flexible and you can also make money with tips.

Airbnb

Do you have an empty room that is just lying there, empty? Why not make that space beautiful and rent it out? You can use sites such as Airbnb to advertise your lovely space and they will bring in customers for you! I have even seen people renting out a tent in their back yard now, it's amazing what is possible if you just get creative.

This is a great way to earn money because it is easy to get up and going and Airbnb takes care of all the booking dates, advertising, and payment!

Rent Out Your Car

Do you have a car that you don't use very often or don't use on specific days of the week? You can use companies such as Turo. Turo allows private car owners to rent out their vehicles via an online and mobile interface in over 56 countries. Think of them as the Airbnb of cars.

This will require very little effort on your part (manage payment, keep the car clean, etc.) and you can earn money from this while you are sitting at home getting ready to start your business!

Teach English As A Second Language

Teaching English to people whose mother tongue is not English has become a massive industry that almost anyone who is fluent in English can do! All you need is a computer and access to the internet. There are many companies that connect native English speakers with people who are looking to learn how to speak English. This is a very popular job and there is a lot of space for you to join it.

Retail Arbitrage

Retail Arbitrage involves buying items for a discounted price and then selling that item for a higher price online, and you keep the difference in the price. For example, you can get a Costco membership or any wholesale club, buy items in bulk and resell them individually on eBay or Amazon.

Or you can even visit outlets and goodwill shops to get discounted items that you can easily resell at a profit.

So here are my top ideas for you to earn some cash to help build funds to start your own hair extensions business! Remember, you do not only have to do one of these and hope that it eventually pays off, you can do as many of them as you like! For example, you can sell unwanted items from your garage and work with DoorDash and run an Airbnb – that would definitely help to build funds superfast for you to start your hair business.

WHAT TO DO NEXT...

I am grateful that you have taken the time to read about my experience and knowledge in the hair industry. I hope by now you are feeling inspired to know that you too can have a successful hair business.

But, Julia, what do I do next? Well, now we need to put all of the pieces together, and to do that I have a **FREE Masterclass** that shows you exactly what steps you need to take from here to get your business started.

What is in the Masterclass?

I must tell you that the masterclass is a huge compliment to this book, and it will fill in any of the pieces that you would ever need to know about if you are wanting to start your hair business the right way, the first time. If you are ready to take the next step and start your own hair business, it is a must-attend.

My goal for you at the end of the masterclass is that you will know exactly what to do next to start your hair business right away.

I will be sharing all the secrets that no one else who is successful in the hair industry is openly giving away for free. In fact, I will be revealing some of the strategies that I share with my private consulting students who pay me $1,000 per hour to help them get started.

Here is the link to register and save your spot ASAP as we only have a limited amount of spots available: WealthyHair.com/Webinar

I cannot guarantee how much longer I will keep this masterclass free because of the value and information shared, so I highly suggest you take advantage and save a spot for the free masterclass right now.

Contact Information

If you ever have any questions or would like to talk to us about anything related to starting your own hair business, you are free to do so! In fact, we would love to hear from you! Below is our contact information.

Email: Help@WealthyHair.com

Call or Text: 1-855-500-4321

Or contact us on the live chat on our website,

WealthyHair.com

www.ingramcontent.com/pod-product-compliance
Lightning Source LLC
Chambersburg PA
CBHW060619200326
41521CB00007B/820